W9-CYA-984

Blue Banner Biography

Keith Urban

Amie Jane Leavitt

P.O. Box 196
Hockessin, Delaware 19707
Visit us on the web: www.mitchelllane.com
Comments? email us: mitchelllane@mitchelllane.com

Mitchell Lane PUBLISHERS

Printing   2   3   4   5   6   7   8   9

Blue Banner Biographies

Akon	Alan Jackson	Alicia Keys
Allen Iverson	Ashanti	Ashlee Simpson
Ashton Kutcher	Avril Lavigne	Bernie Mac
Beyoncé	Bow Wow	Britney Spears
Carrie Underwood	Chris Brown	Chris Daughtry
Christina Aguilera	Christopher Paul Curtis	Ciara
Clay Aiken	Condoleezza Rice	Daniel Radcliffe
David Ortiz	Derek Jeter	Eminem
Eve	Fergie (Stacy Ferguson)	50 Cent
Gwen Stefani	Ice Cube	Jamie Foxx
Ja Rule	Jay-Z	Jennifer Lopez
Jessica Simpson	J. K. Rowling	Johnny Depp
JoJo	Justin Berfield	Justin Timberlake
Kate Hudson	**Keith Urban**	Kelly Clarkson
Kenny Chesney	Lance Armstrong	Lindsay Lohan
Mariah Carey	Mario	Mary J. Blige
Mary-Kate and Ashley Olsen	Michael Jackson	Miguel Tejada
Missy Elliott	Nancy Pelosi	Nelly
Orlando Bloom	P. Diddy	Paris Hilton
Peyton Manning	Queen Latifah	Ron Howard
Rudy Giuliani	Sally Field	Selena
Shakira	Shirley Temple	Tim McGraw
Usher	Zac Efron	

Library of Congress Cataloging-in-Publication Data
Leavitt, Amie Jane.
  Keith Urban / by Amie Jane Leavitt.
     p. cm. — (Blue banner biographies)
  Includes bibliographical references and index.
  ISBN 978-1-58415-619-2 (library bound)
  1. Urban, Keith, 1967 – —Juvenile literature. 2. Country musicians—Australia—Biography—Juvenile literature. I. Title.
ML3930.U83L43 2008
782.421642092—dc22
[B]
                                                                                            2007019684

ABOUT THE AUTHOR: Amie Jane Leavitt is an accomplished author and photographer. She graduated from Brigham Young University as an education major and has since taught all subjects and grade levels in both private and public schools. She is an adventurer who loves to travel the globe in search of interesting story ideas and beautiful places to capture on film. She has written dozens of books for kids, has contributed to online and print media, and has worked as a consultant, writer, and editor for numerous educational publishing and assessment companies. Amie enjoys writing about people who work hard to achieve their dreams. For this reason, she particularly enjoyed researching and writing this book on Keith Urban.

PHOTO CREDITS: Cover—AFP/Getty Images. p. 4—Paul McConnell/Getty Images; p. 7—AFP/Getty Images; p. 10—John Stanton/WireImage; p. 11—G.Weiner/IPOL/Globe Photos, Inc.; p. 15—Frank Micelotta/Getty Images; pp. 16, 22—Rusty Russell/Getty Images; p. 19—Tim Mosenfelder/Getty Images; p. 21—William Thomas Cain/Getty Images; p. 23—Ethan Miller/Getty Images; p. 25—Vince Bucci/Getty Images; p. 26—Ronald C. Modra/Getty Images

PLB, PLB2

Blue Banner Biography

Keith Urban and Nicole Kidman are all smiles on June 26, 2006 — the day after they were married in a traditional Catholic ceremony near Sydney, Australia.

A Grand Event

*I*t was June 25, 2006, in the Cardinal Cerretti (suh-REH-tee) Memorial Chapel in Sydney, Australia. Keith Urban was dressed in a black tuxedo with a white rose on his lapel. He stood nervously waiting by the altar at the end of the chapel's long aisle. "I'm thirty-eight and I've never been married," Keith had recently told a friend. On this evening at twilight, that was going to change. In a few minutes, his bride, in her long veil and ivory chiffon (shih-FAHN) dress, would arrive at the chapel in a vintage Rolls-Royce. Then, after being escorted down the aisle by her father, she and Keith would exchange vows. Soon, the love of Keith's life, actress Nicole Kidman, would be his wife.

Whenever two celebrities get married, it's always a big event. Keith and Nicole's wedding was no different. The chapel was filled with thousands of tiny flickering candles and hundreds of guests. After the couple said "I do," the church bells rang. Then, as the two strolled back down the aisle as husband and wife, the guests showered the couple with silky white rose petals.

A grand white vintage Roll-Royce delivers Nicole Kidman to the chapel where she and Keith Urban will be married.

After the wedding, the party really began. A white reception tent nearby hosted a grand celebration. It was decorated with everything red: roses, carnations, and a red carpet. The guests ate pumpkin ravioli, roast beef, salmon, and mascarpone cake. The music was provided by the sixteen-piece Sydney All Star Big Band.

The highlight of the evening was when Keith serenaded Nicole with his hit song "Making Memories of Us."

When he gave the wedding toast, he told Nicole, "You make me feel like I'm becoming the man I was always meant to be." A guest at the event said, "He was absolutely focused on her, and she was crying and everybody was crying."

Keith and Nicole were happy that their close friends and family could be there to celebrate with them. Keith's parents were there. His older brother, Shane, was his best man. Nicole's parents were there too. Her sister, Antonia, was her matron of honor, and Nicole's daughter, Isabella, was one of her bridesmaids. Her son, Connor, was an usher. Keith was happy that both of Nicole's children were there to celebrate this special day with them.

The couple wanted to share their wedding day with others, so they asked their friends and family not to buy them gifts. Instead, they asked them to donate money to Sydney Children's Hospital.

After the wedding, Keith and Nicole slipped away on their honeymoon to the islands of French Polynesia. Their lives together were beginning right where Keith's had started — on a beautiful warm island in the South Pacific.

The couple asked their friends and family to donate money to Sydney Children's Hospital.

Farm Boy from the Land Down Under

*I*n the Maori (MAH-oh-ree) language, *Whangarei* (WAHN-gair-ee) means "Bountiful Land." Located two hours north of Auckland on New Zealand's North Island, the place is indeed beautiful. It has sparkling waterfalls, soft sand beaches, lush green forests, and aqua-blue bays. In this seaside community where "the city meets the sea," Keith Lionel Urban was born on October 26, 1967.

Keith is the second son of Robert and Marienne Urban. Their first child, Shane, was born two years earlier. Keith was named after Keith Haub, a famous horserace caller from New Zealand. His middle name, Lionel, comes from an uncle on his mother's side. Sometimes Keith's family would just call him their favorite nickname. Since he was the second and youngest child, Keith was given the nickname "Sub-urban."

The Urban family would spend the next two years in New Zealand. When Keith was two years old, they moved to Brisbane on the eastern shore of Australia.

"We moved around a lot in the city of Brisbane when I was very young," Keith told an Australian reporter in 2005. "Then my dad decided it was time to get back to his rural upbringing. He bought a property in a place called Caboolture [kah-BOOL-chur], a farming town about an hour north of Brisbane. We moved up there and lived on this 12-acre farm."

Bob wanted his family to live off the land and be self-sufficient, so they planted crops and raised animals. The entire family helped with chores and worked the land. "I'm very comfortable around cattle," says Keith. "I can ride a horse alright. I can collect eggs and I can clean out a pigsty." He would even help milk the cows, but, he says, "I wasn't very good at it."

Keith would even help milk the cows, but, he says, "I wasn't very good at it."

Bob Urban liked the farming lifestyle and living in a rural area. He also enjoyed listening to country music and had a huge collection of records from American country music artists. "I grew up with all these country records in my dad's collection," Keith says. He listened to such artists as Don Williams, Charley Pride, Dolly Parton, Glen Campbell, Jim Reeves, Johnny Cash, and Ronnie Milsap. "My dad took me to see Tom T. Hall when I was six," Keith says. "About a year later, Johnny Cash toured Australia. My dad took me to see him. Those were the first two concerts I ever saw."

While in Caboolture, the Urbans signed up for a local Country Music Club. This was a social club for fans of

Keith is known for his skills as a guitarist. He began playing when he was six and has always felt at home holding a guitar.

country music. "I thought everybody was in a Country Music Club," says Keith. "It's like a lifestyle in Australia. Families all join these little clubs, and they'd have events once a month. And then once a year all the Country Music Clubs in Australia would get together in one town and compete, club to club." He grew to love everything about country music at a very young age.

At home, Keith listened to his dad's records so often that he practically had the tunes memorized. As the vinyl records spun on the player, he would study the information

Keith started out as a musician in Australia. Then he moved to Nashville, Tennessee, to see if he could make it in Music City, USA. By 2001 he was beginning to see success there.

on the back of the covers. *Recorded in Nashville, Tennessee*, was boldly printed at the bottom of each cardboard sleeve. At age seven, Keith came to a conclusion: "That's where you go to make records." At that moment, he made a decision that would affect the rest of his life. He declared, "When I'm old enough to get there, I'll get there." Later, in 2001, Keith said, "I never faltered from that. I feel like I'm pursuing a destiny as opposed to chasing a dream."

While older brother Shane enjoyed spending his time at the beach surfing, Keith preferred listening to country music and practicing his instruments. "I grew up playing American country," Keith says. At age three, he learned how to play the ukulele. By the age of six, he had graduated to a more difficult stringed instrument: the acoustic guitar. "I remember holding that guitar at a very young age and it just felt so comfortable, so natural," he says.

Later, Keith would learn to play the mandolin, the piano, the banjo, and many other instruments. He didn't just play them like any average young kid would do. He was so good that by the age of eight, he was entering talent competitions and winning them.

One group that had a big impact on Keith during his growing-up years was the British band Dire Straits. Unlike the other music he listened to, this band didn't play country music. They played classic rock. Keith bought the group's records and learned how to play their songs. Then he began combining some of this rock-style music into his own country solos. Keith really admired the talent of one band member in particular. "Mark Knopfler [NOF-ler] has inspired me as a guitarist," Keith told a reporter in 2001. This inspiration led to Keith's developing his own style—a unique blend of rock-and-roll-style guitar and country.

> **One group that had a big impact on Keith during his growing-up years was the British band Dire Straits.**

Making His Mark on Music City, USA

*O*ver the next four years, Keith continued practicing and performing his music. When he was twelve, he joined a small band. They played regularly at local pubs. By the time he was in his mid-teens, he was making good money as a musician and enjoying the lifestyle of an entertainer. At age fifteen, he decided to quit school and play his music full-time.

Keith spent the next few years traveling all over eastern Australia with his three-piece band. They performed in pubs and clubs in both small towns and big cities. One evening, they performed in a club in Australia's most populated city, Sydney. A fellow Aussie country guitarist and songwriter, Bill Chambers, was in the audience that night. He said, "It was one of the best gigs we'd ever seen. I just couldn't believe how good he [Keith] was. Of course he's a good-looking guy and he's got a great voice, but to be able to play those guitar licks at the same time as you sing—I was just awestruck."

Bill Chambers wasn't the only person who was impressed with Keith Urban's musical talent. In 1990, EMI

Music in Australia signed Urban to a record contract. His first solo album, titled *Keith Urban*, was released in 1991. Four of the songs on this album hit number one on Australia's country music charts.

Urban had done quite well for himself in Australia. Yet ever since his childhood, his dream was to move to the Mecca of Country Music: Nashville, Tennessee. "I inherited this kind of love for the American dream," he said in 2005. "I fell in love with the music, the cars, and the whole idea of America." So, in 1992, Urban made his big leap. He boarded a plane and traveled nearly 9,000 miles away from his friends and family in Australia to move to Music City, USA.

He boarded a plane and traveled nearly 9,000 miles away from his friends and family in Australia to move to Music City, USA.

Nashville was a lot different than Urban had expected. "I was shocked how small Nashville was. I was expecting a much bigger city," he told John Mellencamp in an interview in 2006. Even though Nashville was a small town, Urban still felt like a little fish in a big pond.

There weren't too many Australian country music singers in America. In fact, Urban was probably one of the only ones. "It was probably hard for people in Nashville to accept an Australian," Marienne Urban told a reporter in 2001. Not only does Keith not sound like other country music stars when he talks (he speaks with an Australian accent), he also does not dress the same. He wears baseball caps instead of big Stetson cowboy hats. He has shaggy highlighted blond

Keith and his mother, Marienne Urban, attended the 34th Annual CMA Awards in 2000. Keith's first solo album, Keith Urban, *had been released just a few months before.*

Keith strums one of his ballads during the Brooks & Dunn set at the 2006 CMA Music Festival in Nashville.

hair. Some of his friends even say that he is a "rock star in disguise" because he looks more like Jon Bon Jovi than he does the typical country music star.

Urban really struggled when he first came to Nashville. "I could only take so much rejection. Especially when you've paid your dues back home. Then you come here and you're no one," he said. He was all alone Nashville. He missed his family and friends. He missed the ocean and the laid-back way of life in Australia.

Even so, Urban was bound and determined not to give up. He had come to America to make his mark, and he was not going to leave until he did so. Urban formed a band called Four Wheel Drive. Later on he renamed it The Ranch. Urban sang lead and played guitar. Peter Clarke played drums, and Jerry Flowers sang harmony and played the bass. This three-piece band paid their dues. They played at small, dingy bars and clubs. They entertained at summertime festivals, chili cook-offs, and barbecues. Finally, all their hard work paid off. Their first record, titled *The Ranch*, was released by Capitol Records in 1997.

Finally, all their hard work paid off. Their first record, titled The Ranch, was released by Capitol Records in 1997.

This would also be the group's only album. A year after the album's release, The Ranch decided to split up. "The band was getting to the point where it just didn't make sense to continue on," Urban told a reporter in 1999. The three members were going in different directions with their musical careers. "I thought this was the perfect time for us to part ways and move on and look back at The Ranch as being a good, fun project," he said. Pete moved on to play drums with the group Big House. Jerry started writing more of his own music and performing with the Dixie Chicks. And Keith would begin his solo career.

Hard Times Make You Stronger

*U*rban was excited about going solo, yet it would be a difficult time in his life. "Relationship issues and some personal demons I was dealing with, and life just came barreling down on me all in one year," he said. "Everything went wrong and I went through a black period in my life."

Urban had made some really poor choices when he first arrived in Nashville. He was lonely and didn't have a family to spend time with when he was discouraged. He got involved in drugs. He knew this was a bad mistake, but it was hard for him to stop. Soon he became addicted. In 1998, he knew he had to get help, so he checked himself into the Cumberland Heights treatment center in Nashville. There he was able to get help from medical professionals.

At this time, Urban also had some problems with his vocal cords. He had performed too much over the previous few years, and his voice didn't get a chance to rest. His vocal cords became strained. He had to get special treatments from a doctor to help him heal them.

Not only can Urban play the guitar, he's also talented on other stringed instruments, including the banjo. Even with all his talents, he has fought personal demons that have led to drug and alcohol addiction.

Sometimes it seems that everything goes bad at once. That's what it must have felt like for Urban during this time of his life. Not only did he have the troubles mentioned above, but he also had problems with his long-term girlfriend. He and Laura Sigler had dated since 1992, but by 1998, their relationship was really rocky. They would date and break up over and over again for the next few years.

> *Hard times can get a person down or make the person stronger. Keith chose to gain strength from his troubles.*

Hard times can get a person down or make the person stronger. Keith chose to gain strength from his troubles. After he managed to get his life in order, his career took off. He was asked to perform guitar with Garth Brooks on *Double Live*. The Dixie Chicks also invited him to play with them on their album *Fly*.

In the late 1990s, Capitol Records signed Urban as a solo artist. In 1999, his first solo single, "It's a Love Thing," was released. This song received rave reviews across the country. A radio producer in Salt Lake City, Utah, said that year, "I think it's the best sounding song on the air right now. I love it. He is absolutely what we need right now. He loves music. He has a base in country music. He's the best guitarist I've ever heard, and his voice is incredible."

Urban's self-titled album, which he coproduced, was released in 1999. He also wrote three of the songs and cowrote six others. Most of the album is about relationships, focusing on what is good in them. The relationships in his

Urban entertains during the Live 8 Philadelphia charity concert in 2005. Throughout his career, Urban has donated to or performed in benefits for many worthy causes.

songs aren't just between people—some of them are between a person and a higher power. One of these songs, "But for the Grace of God," was written with Charlotte Caffey and Jane Weidlin, two singers from the Go-Gos. It soared to the number one spot on the Billboard charts.

In 2001, Urban performed on the Brooks & Dunn Neon Circus Tour. Later that year, the Academy of Country Music Awards named him the Top New Male Vocalist, and he received the Country Music Association's Horizon Award. Nashville, and the entire country music scene, was finally taking notice of Keith Urban. "I think it took me a while to convince Nashville that what I do is genuine and my heart's in the right place, and I love country music," he stated in 2001.

Urban released *Golden Road* in 2002; it went triple platinum in the United States, which means that it sold over three million copies. In 2004, his next album, *Be Here,*

Keith received the Country Music Association Top Male Vocalist Award for the first time in 2004. He was the first non-American to win this award.

was released. This album was nominated for the recording industry's highest honor, a Grammy Award. It was also named the Album of the Year in 2005 by the Academy of Country Music. In 2006, Urban released *Love, Pain, and the Whole Crazy Thing*. He said that this album is "the sound of being happy with my life and passionate about the music that I'm making." The first song on the album, "Once in a Lifetime," was nominated for another Grammy Award.

Keith Urban played nationally, opening for fellow country musician Kenny Chesney. Keith would tour solo in 2007 during his Love, Pain & The Whole Crazy Thing *World Tour.*

Besides Grammys, Urban has received many other awards. In 2004, he became the first non-American to receive a Country Music Award for Male Vocalist of the Year. He continued to win this award in 2005 and 2006. In 2005, he was the first non-American male to receive the Country Music's Entertainer of the Year Award.

Urban kept touring. He was the opening act for his pal Kenny Chesney in 2004. He toured in his Alive concert in 2005 and his Still Alive concert in 2006.

Keith Urban's musical career has truly exceeded the expectations of many people. By 2007, he had sold over five million albums and had eight top five singles in the United States.

CHAPTER 5

G'Day, L.A.

*U*rban's music career has been very important to him, yet he knew there was more to life than just a career. A reporter once asked him if he wanted to get married and have a family of his own. Urban replied, "Absolutely. I thought it would have happened sooner than it has, quite frankly."

Urban had started dating Laura Sigler in 1992. Even though they had rough times, the two had dated on and off for eight years. In 2001, Keith asked her to marry him. Before they could tie the knot, they broke up for good in 2002. Urban then dated a model named Niki Taylor for a few years. After their breakup in 2004, he decided to just focus on his career for a while. He was busy touring and was rarely home anyway. "No time for a relationship," he told a reporter in December 2004.

Yet single life didn't last for long. In January 2005, he was invited to an event called G'Day L.A. This annual dinner honored Australian celebrities in America. Keith

Country singer Keith Urban attends the Penfolds Gala Dinner, the kickoff event for G'Day L.A.: Australia Week 2005. At this event, Keith would meet the love of his life.

was honored that night for his achievements in the entertainment industry. Another Aussie, Nicole Kidman, was also honored that night. This was the first time these two entertainers had met.

Soon after the event, Keith and Nicole started dating. They didn't want reporters to know about their relationship, so they tried to keep it secret. Even so, by July of that year, everyone knew they were together. The couple was seen vacationing in the New York Hamptons. They were also spotted strolling the streets of Nashville. By November, it was obvious that the couple was serious. Keith hosted

Nicole Kidman proudly shows off the stunning diamond ring Keith gave her. Keith says being with Nicole has brought balance to his life. "I was always about my work. I was focused on that from a young age. It's only recently that the personal side of my life has blossomed."

Thanksgiving at his house in Nashville for his family and Nicole's family. Nicole began sporting a big diamond ring.

Just a few months after Keith and Nicole were married, Keith started having a difficult time again. He realized that he needed help, so he checked himself into the Betty Ford Center in California. This clinic helps people who have addictions to alcohol and other drugs. Urban felt terrible about the pain his relapse had caused his family. "One can never let one's guard down on recovery, and I'm afraid I have. I deeply regret the hurt this has caused Nicole and the ones that love and support me," he said.

Through it all, Nicole stood by his side. Part of their wedding vows said "through sickness and in health" and "through good times and bad." Nicole took her vows seriously and wanted to be there to help Keith through this hard time. "With the strength and unwavering support I am blessed to have from my wife, family and friends, I am determined and resolved to a positive outcome," Urban said in October 2006.

Urban spent several months in rehab and was finally released in January 2007. Once he finished his recovery program, he planned to tour again. He had concerts lined up throughout the United States and Europe beginning in February 2007. He would play music from his latest album, *Love, Pain, and the Whole Crazy Thing*.

Of course, his fans were delighted that he was well enough to perform again — and so was Keith. "Music is like air to me," he says. "It's like breathing."

Music is definitely Keith's passion. "I love what I do, I always have," he says. "I've kind of had a renewed love for it in the last few years, and it's a wonderful blessing."

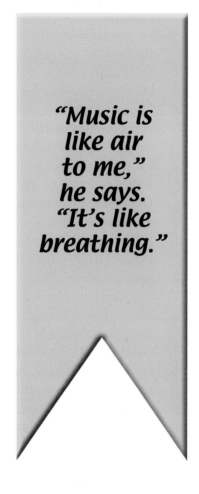

"Music is like air to me," he says. "It's like breathing."

Hopefully, for the sake of country music fans everywhere, there will be many more years of beautiful music from Keith Urban. With his determination and work ethic, chances are good that this Aussie is here to stay. G'Day mate!

1967   Keith Lionel Urban is born on October 26 in Whangarei, New Zealand.
1969   He moves with his family to Brisbane, Australia.
1970   Keith starts playing the ukulele.
1971   His family settles on a farm in Caboolture, Australia.
1973   He starts playing the guitar.
1974   He decides he wants to move to Nashville when he grows up.
1975   He begins competing in talent competitions and winning.
1983   Keith drops out of high school to tour with his band full-time.
1988   He starts a three-piece band and tours eastern Australia.
1990   Keith is signed by EMI in Australia.
1991   His first solo album sees four number ones on Australia's country music charts.
1992   He moves to Nashville, Tennessee, and forms the band Four Wheel Drive, which is eventually named The Ranch. He begins dating Laura Sigler.
1997   *The Ranch* is released by Capitol Records.
1998   The Ranch splits up. Keith checks into Cumberland Heights treatment center in Nashville; after recovery, he performs with Garth Brooks on *Double Live*.
1999   His self-titled American debut is released by Capitol Records; it has three top five hits. He performs with the Dixie Chicks on *Fly*.
2001   He proposes to Laura Sigler, receives award for Top New Male Vocalist at the Academy of Country Music Awards; receives Country Music Association Horizon Award; and tours with Brooks & Dunn on Neon Circus Tour.
2002   He releases *Golden Road*. He and Laura Sigler break up for good.
2004   He releases *Be Here* and tours with Kenny Chesney. He receives a Country Music Award for Male Vocalist of the Year.
2005   Keith meets Nicole Kidman at G'Day L.A. in January. *Be Here* is named album of the year by Academy of Country Music Awards and nominated for a Grammy Award. *Livin' Right Now* DVD is released. Urban receives two Country Music Awards (Male Vocalist of the Year and Entertainer of the Year). He tours with his Alive concert.

2006   Keith and Nicole Kidman marry on June 25 in Australia. Keith checks into Betty Ford Center in California in October. *Love, Pain, and the Whole Crazy Thing* is released in November. For the third year in a row, he is named Male Vocalist of the Year by Country Music Association. He tours with Still Alive concert.

2007   He completes alcohol rehabilitation program at the Betty Ford Center in January. He begins touring Europe and U.S. in February.

DISCOGRAPHY

Albums

1991   *Keith Urban* (Australian release)
1997   *The Ranch*
1999   *Keith Urban*
2002   *Golden Road*
2004   *In the Ranch* (reissue)
2004   *Be Here*
2005   *Days Go By* (UK only release)
2006   *Love, Pain, and the Whole Crazy Thing*

Awards

2004   Country Music Association (CMA) — Male Vocalist of the Year
2005   Grammy — Best Male Country Vocal Performance
         Country Music Television (CMT) Music Award — Video of the Year
         CMA — Male Vocalist of the Year and Entertainer of the Year
         Academy of Country Music (ACM) — Top Male Vocalist
2006   CMA — Male Vocalist of the Year
         ACM — Top Male Vocalist
         CMT Music Award — Video of the Year

Books

Although there are no other books for teens about Keith Urban, you might enjoy these country music Blue Banner Biographies from Mitchell Lane Publishers:

Alan Jackson, by Jennifer Torres
Carrie Underwood, by Kathleen Tracy
Kenny Chesney, by Michelle Medlock Adams
Tim McGraw, by Michelle Medlock Adams

Works Consulted

Abel, Olivia. "What to Like About Keith." *People*, August 15, 2005. p. 20.
　　Bullins, Strother. "Kenny Chesney and Keith Urban." *Mix*, July 2004.
　　p. 82.
Frost, Caroline. "Faces of the Week: Keith Urban." *BBC News*, June 23,
　　2006.
Fuoco, Christina. "Live Daily Interview: Keith Urban." *Live Daily*.
　　http://www.livedaily.com/interviews/liveDaily_Interview_Keith_
　　Urban-5467.html?t=6
"Golden Road." *Warner Music Australia*. http://www.warnermusic.com.
　　au/artist,w_artist,103172
Hunter, Lauren. "Aussie Keith Urban's Success 'Destiny.' " *CNN.com/
　　Entertainment*. February 19, 2001. http://archives.cnn.com/2001/
　　SHOWBIZ/Music/02/19/keith.urban/
John, Elton. "Keith Urban." *Interview*, October 2006. pp. 134–136.
　　"Keith Urban and Johnno: Saturday Night Country." *ABC Online*.
　　March 3, 2005. http://www.abc.net.au/snc/stories/s1310341.htm
"Keith Urban Enters Rehab." Associated Press, October 20, 2006.
　　http://wcbstv.com/entertainment/entertainment_story_293182715.
　　html
"Keith Urban," *Muzica*. http://music.moldova.org/band/eng/332/
"Keith Urban." *People*, November 13, 2000. p.165.
"Keith Urban." *People*, November 15, 2004. p.80.
"Keith Urban." *People*, November 8, 2006. p. 48.
"Keith Urban: Awards," *Country Music Television*: http://www.cmt.com/
　　artists/az/urban_keith/awards.jhtml
"Keith Urban: Biography," *Country Music Television*: http://www.cmt.
　　com/artists/az/urban_keith/bio.jhtml

"Keith Urban Interview." February 5, 2001. http://countrymusic.about.com/library/blkuinterview.htm

Keogh, Sue. "Keith Urban, In the Ranch," *BBC Folk and Country Review*. http://www.bbc.co.uk/music/release/nfmq/

Lopez, Molly. "What Was Your Childhood Nickname?" *People*, April 11, 2005. p. 146.

Mansfield, Stephanie. "Up and Down Under." *USA Weekend*, November 4, 2001.

Mellencamp, John. "Keith Urban." *Interview*, August 2006. pp. 122–123. *Official Keith Urban Website*. http://www.keithurban.net

"Nicole Says, 'I Do.' " *Tribute*, July/August 2006. p. 54.

Price, Deborah Evans. "Aussie Keith Urban Debuts on Capitol." *Billboard*, September 25, 1999. p. 43.

Price, Deborah Evans. "Country Goes Urban." *Billboard*, November 26, 2005. p. 14.

Skanse, Richard. "Keith Urban's Slow and Steady Race to Be Here." http://countrymusic.about.com/od/keithurban/a/blkurban_cma.htm

Smith, Hazel. "Hot Dish: Keith Urban Is Too Busy for Romance." *Country Music Television*. December 20, 2004. http://www.cmt.com/news/articles/1495025/12172004/urban_keith.jhtml

Tauber, Michelle. "Nicole and Keith's Magic Night." *People*, July 10, 2006. pp. 58–63.

Thompson, Jenn. "Drunk on Oz Cheer." *Variety*, January 24, 2005. p. 60.

"Whangarei New Zealand," New Zealand's Information Network. http://www.newzealandnz.co.nz/whangarei/

Willman, Chris. "Keith Urban 101." *Entertainment Weekly*, December 9, 2005. p. 18.

Web sites

Keith Urban Official Website
    http://www.keithurban.net/

Country Music Television: Keith Urban
    http://www.cmt.com/artists/az/urban_keith/artist.jhtml

INDEX